CONTE

MY DOG

A Poem to Share

WRITTEN BY DOROTHY AVERY
ILLUSTRATED BY FRASER WILLIAMSON

Some dogs are fluffy.
Some dogs are hairy.
Some dogs are cuddly.
Some dogs are scary.

Some dogs like running.
Some dogs like walking.
Some dogs like swimming.
Some dogs like stalking.

But the best dog of all
Is the one that I know.
My dog goes with me
Wherever I go!

WRONG DAY, MARCUS

Written by Stuart Payne
6 Illustrated by Annabel Craighead

On Monday,
Shirley caught the ferry
to work. So did Marcus.

"The dog's with me,"
she said to the boatman.

On Tuesday,
Marcus sailed with Shirley
again. He barked
at the seagulls
as they crossed the harbour.

"Come on, Marcus,"
Shirley said,
getting off the ferry.

On Wednesday,
Shirley had lunch
with Marcus in the park.
Then she went back to work.

On Thursday,
Marcus was cold
on the ferry deck.
His ears drooped.
His eyes looked sad.

The boatman found him
a cosy spot in the cabin.

On Friday,
Marcus lay in the sun.
He watched the pigeons.

Shirley finished work late.
They nearly missed
the ferry back home.

On Saturday,
it was Shirley's day off work.
When Shirley got up,
she called and called Marcus,
but he didn't come.

Then Shirley had an idea.
She rang the boatman.

"Yes," he said, "your dog
is here with me.
I'll look after him."

On Sunday,
Marcus sailed home.

Shirley said,
"Right boat, Marcus.
Right place, Marcus.
But *wrong day, Marcus!*"

21

CLEVER
Hamburger

WRITTEN BY
MARGARET MAHY

ILLUSTRATED BY
RODNEY McRAE

Mum stopped the car outside the big shop.

"Jane, help Tom out of his car seat," said Mum.

Tom cried.

"Poor boy. It's been a long day for him. He wants to sleep," said Mum.

Hamburger, the dog,
did not want to sleep.
He wanted to go shopping.

"Stay there, Hamburger!
We won't be long!"
said Mum.

Tom cried again.

"Poor tired boy,"
said Mum.

They went into the shop
to buy a pair
of shoes for Jane.
The blue ones were too big.
The pink ones were too small.
The green ones with the
rainbow laces were just right.

When Mum and Jane
had bought the shoes,
they looked around for Tom.
Tom was gone.
Where was Tom?

Mum and Jane looked
upstairs and downstairs.
They looked in
all the lifts.

"I'll have to call
the police," said Mum.
"Tom is lost."

"Let's try Hamburger,"
said Jane. "He's just
outside in the car."

Hamburger was happy
to be out of the car.

"Hamburger!" said Mum.
"Find Tom!"

"Hamburger!" said Jane.
"Find Tom!"

Hamburger put his nose
to the ground and ran
this way and that.

Mum and Jane followed him
through the big shop,
right to one of the soft,
flowery beds.

There on the bed was Tom.

"Hamburger," said Mum.
"You are the cleverest dog
in the world."

Dogs,
Cats,
AND
Mice

Written by May Nelson
Illustrated by Fraser Williamson

Once upon a time, dogs, cats, and mice were friends. Then, one day, the dogs had to go away on a trip.

"We have some important papers," they told the cats. "Will you look after them for us?"

"Yes," said the cats. "We will keep them safe for you."

When the dogs had gone, the cats said, "We have nowhere to keep the papers. Let's give them to the mice."

"Will you look after these papers for us?" the cats asked the mice. "Will you keep them safe?"

"Yes," said the mice. "We'll look after them for you."

Winter came.
The mice were cold.
They nibbled at the papers
and made little nests
to keep themselves warm.

Then, one day,
the dogs came back.
"We've come for our papers,"
they said to the cats.

"We had nowhere safe
to keep them," said the cats.
"We gave them to the mice.
We'll get them for you."

43

The cats went to the mice.
"The dogs are back,"
they said. "We've come
for the papers."

When they saw
what the mice had done,
the cats were very angry.
They chased every mouse
they saw.

45

The cats went back
to the dogs.
"The mice did not look
after your papers," they said.
"The mice were cold,
so they made them into nests."

The dogs were very angry
with the cats.
They chased every cat
they saw.

From that day on,
dogs have chased cats,
and cats have chased mice.
They have never been
friends again!